INSIGHTS INTO ADDICTION AND RECOVERY

by

Tariq A. Shabazz

ISBN: 0-7596-5654-1

This book is printed on acid free paper.

1stBooks – rev. 01/31/02

Address all inquiries to:

Tariq Adib Shabazz
P.O. Box 44293
Philadelphia Pa. 19144
E-Mail Tashabazz@aol.com

Published in the United States of America

Acknowledgments

I can never thank Allah (God) enough for blessing me with the opportunity to complete this book. I am forever grateful for the numerous people that helped play a part in developing me into the man that I am today. This book is dedicated to my parents (my father, the late John Jennings and my mother, Mrs. Lillie Mae Jennings). My parents always supported me through thick and thin, always giving me their love and wise advice. I give a special thanks to my wife Elvera Mannaan Shabazz who has been in my corner despite all odds. I must also acknowledge my long time friend, herb specialist and entrepreneur, Mr. Boris C. Barcliff. Mr. Barcliff was very helpful with the editing of this book. This task would have been extremely difficult to accomplish without his support. Lastly, I would like to thank the numerous family members and friends (too numerous to mention) who have encouraged and supported me throughout my life to do the right thing. I will remain forever grateful for their support.

Contents

Introduction

This book, "Insights Into Addiction and Recovery" became a reality after I took a great interest in the ill effects of drug use. I began this project in 1993 by conducting interviews with men and women who were recovering from their addiction to a wide range of drugs and alcohol abuse.

I was once addicted to drugs and alcohol. It was only by the grace of the Creator that I became free of this devastating and diabolical trap of Satan. I can not imagine where I would be today without the help of the Creator. I felt an inspired obligation to write this book and feel strongly that some people will benefit from the life experiences of those who participated in this project. I wish to extend a heart-felt thank you to them at this time. I did not use the actual names of the participants in order to protect their true identities. My interest in the ill effects of alcohol and drug abuse grew when I started working in Human Services in 1987. I came in contact with many people who were addicted to drugs and alcohol. My concern and interest in drug and alcohol abuse increased tremendously.

Today we find almost every family touched by a member addicted to drugs. Some families, unfortunately, have more than one member who suffers this addiction. It is important for the readers to understand that when the term drugs is used this includes alcohol. Alcohol has been greatly overlooked because of its acceptance and legalization in our society. We should not delude ourselves: **ALCOHOL IS A VERY DANGEROUS DRUG.**

This project consists of a number of interviews with men and women of different ethnic and religious persuasions. These interviews with the participants were given while they were in recovery. Due to the realities of life, it is quite possible that some of the participants may have returned to using drugs or lost their lives since giving their interviews. My experiences with the observance of addicts bear out this possibility.

The emphasis should be placed on the information that the participants have offered while living a drug free life. The interviews have been condensed and focus is placed on the most pertinent information. The contents of this book may be interpreted by some to be extraordinary and painful. It is a blessing that these men and women are alive considering what they have gone through. If one person's life is improved as a result of this book, it will have made this effort worthwhile.

The Catastrophe-A Blessing in Disguise

Interview of September 9, 1993

Ali is an African American male in his early 40's. He is married and has four children. He has been free from his addiction to drugs and alcohol for over 10 years. He came from a family of seven children. His father went to work at an early age and was unable to pursue an education. Ali's mother did not have to work and did her best to raise her children.

Ali was an excellent student during his early school days and appeared to be well on his way to a promising education. Unfortunately for

Ali, things began to change as his life became dramatically disrupted. That disruption was a change in his environment. He had to move to a new neighborhood. The new neighborhood meant unfamiliar people as well as a new challenge for Ali and his family. It did not take Ali long to become acquainted with a street gang and experience his first exposure to alcohol at the tender age of 12. Ali still maintained his education but the seed for his desire of alcohol had been planted and that desire grew. It was a matter of time before his interest in school started declining. Ali found himself expelled from school at the age of 15 after numerous suspensions.

He was involved with criminal activity and his alcohol problem surged out of control. His anti-social behavior ranged from petit larceny to strong- arm robbery. He was well acquainted with the ways of the street. It did not take him long before he was arrested and sentenced to a juvenile reformatory. The reform school did little to address his alcohol problem. Ali learned other ways to get high. He was released after serving his sentence and within a matter of days he returned to his old ways. The criminal and alcohol activity continued until he was again arrested and sent to prison. While in prison, he became acquainted with members of the Nation of Islam and became a follower of The Honorable Elijah Muhammad. Things were coming along okay for Ali. His newly found faith gave him the strength and courage to fight his addiction. He was released and was striving to be a productive member of society. Unfortunately, Ali became acquainted with negative young peers who had influences on him. They were determined to do things that they knew were contrary to the new teachings in Islam that he had learned. It was not long before Ali found himself imprisoned again.

He became involved with learning more about the religion of Islam and eventually became a Muslim who follows the Holy Qur'an and the traditions of Prophet Muhammad (peace and blessings be upon him) of 1400 years ago. He maintained this practice after his release from prison. Ali was doing fine until he became re-aquatinted with bad influences. He started getting high and doing things that were contrary to his religion. This struggle continued until he learned how to change his heart by putting the Creator first in his life. Things began to become clear to him now. He finally began to understand the many things that his parents and friends tried to tell him. One of the sayings of one of the Prophets of God became crystal clear in his head as if it were a revelation. That saying was, **"It was better to be alone than to be in the mist of bad company; and it is better to be in good company than to be alone."** Ali remembered this saying well because when he first read it, a light seemed to have clicked on his head and the puzzle to his life seemed to be solved. Ali realized that for most of his life his troubles were created when he followed those who were a bad influence on him. He finally came to the realization that he had never learned to follow his own heart. His very first drink, his first crime and the negativity he learned stemmed from those harmful influences in his life.

Ali constantly remembers the violence and the harsh reality of prison life. To maintain a drug free life, Ali avoids being in the company of negative people and makes it his priority to focus on thinking positive. He works hard at his place of employment and on himself. He keeps an open mind and tries to learn from anyone who has something positive to offer him. He is very active within his community. Ali also learned to look at the success of others and incorporates anything that is helpful into his life.

My Children-The Road to Recovery

Interview of September 20, 1993

Marie is a 46-year-old African American female married with four children. At the time of this interview, she was clean and sober for a little over 10 years. Marie recalls that around the age of 10 or 11 she was exposed to alcohol. She remembers her parents having a party. Marie along with her sisters were sneaking drinks. She stated that she never really liked to drink but did so because it was available. It was just something to do at the time.

Marie's family was poor and many people would come to her parents' home to drink and pass the time. She was a girl that enjoyed experimenting with new things. She recalls that on one occasion one of her mother's friends offered her some money if she would drink a certain amount of corn liquor. Marie drank the alcohol without giving it a second thought. On another occasion her father had offered her something to drink although he did advise her that it would probably be too strong for her. She did not take heed to her father's advice and drank it anyway. Her father advice was an obvious contradiction that adversely affected her life.

It was clear that Marie's addiction to alcohol came as a result of her exposure to alcohol and her addictive personality. The years went by and Marie became introduced to other drugs such as marijuana, PCP (phencyclidine) and amphetamines. She had ample opportunity to experience these illegal substances. Her boyfriend and best girlfriend were drug dealers. It became very easy for Marie to get the drugs she wanted from either of them. Marie can recall that while she was in her addiction she trusted someone whom she considered to be her friend. He allowed her to be taken advantage of by others sexually while she was intoxicated.

In another situation she remembers herself getting into fights and being disrespectful of many people she came in contact with. Her drinking was the root cause of a lot of abnormal behavior that she was displaying. She sought to change her trouble life. Marie gives credit to the Creator for giving her a new found interest in her children and giving her strength to pull away from drugs and alcohol. In essence she was given a new lease on life. Her rekindled interest in her children made her realize that the road to recovery started with her children.

Marie continues to diligently practice her faith in the religion of Islam. In her conclusion, she would like to stress the importance of looking at the lifestyles of people who are using drugs. She is conscious of the people she associates with. She cautions teenagers to stay in school and stay off the streets. Most of all she believes people should strive to be the best that they can be.

The Subway to Change

Interview of October 7, 1993

Byron is a 37 year old single African American male with no children. At the time of this interview he was drug free for 4 months. Byron was extremely addicted to crack cocaine in the recent past, but was cold sober during this interview. He was born in North Philadelphia and raised with five siblings. He also had numerous half brothers and sisters in what was considered a dysfunctional family. His father was an alcoholic and his mother a moderate drinker.

He remembers many of his relatives being addicted to drugs and alcohol. His first experience with drugs came about during his teenage years. Byron felt what led to his addiction was the need to medicate himself from the various problems he was having in his life. He expressed the feeling that he did not receive the proper amount of love and nurturing from his parents. Byron, during his addiction, experimented with a number of illegal substances until he finally became addicted to crack cocaine. While in his addiction, he manipulated women, as do many men when they find an unwitting enabler. Despite Byron's manipulative ways and street smarts, he occasionally found himself eating his meals at dumpsites. He would steal, lie and betray the trust of his family and friends. Byron simply states it this way, **"I dare to care not of how I got my drug (which was crack cocaine). I wanted it, how I wanted it, now! You know they speak of the fact that the disease of addiction is cunning and baffling. It can never be cured. It can only be put in remission like cancer."**

Byron remembers experiencing pain, despair, loneliness and a general need of wanting to be loved. When he couldn't receive the love he so badly desired, he returned to his comfort zone, which was crack cocaine. While he was in therapy he dealt with a lot of internal issues such as the hatred he had for his father and the inability to get along with his family. He shockingly recalls seeing junkies inject narcotics into their genitals. He also

13

remembers many scary incidents that occurred while he and his associates were using drugs. One of the men that were getting high with them became delusional and jumped out of the window. He was fortunate that he only broke his leg.

On another occasion one of the men he was getting high with pulled out a gun because he had become paranoid. It goes without saying that all of his colleagues fled not withstanding their altered states of mind. It was only through God's mercy that the man did not injure or kill anyone. Byron related that on another occasion while having sex with a prostitute in a park he caught a severe case of poison ivy. This illustrates the shameful, irresponsible actions of an individual caught in the clutches of the sinister grip of illegal drugs. He states that out of all the drugs he has used, crack cocaine was the worst. He puts it this way, **"crack cocaine has all but destroyed me and I truly believe that if I didn't take charge of myself during a brief moment of sanity and sought therapy I wouldn't be sitting here today at this interview. Crack cocaine is a very devastating drug because of its potency. It doesn't care who you are or what you are capable of doing. It will literally sap you of all your strength. It will make women do things that I didn't know women were capable of doing. It made me participate in unspeakable things with women I didn't know I was capable of doing. I would even allow guys to perform felatio on me in exchange for drugs. Of course,**

when one is under the influence of drugs he may do things contrary to his basic character. I would also steal, which is something that I am adamant against. I sold people phony drugs, deceiving them to believe they were real. Friends trusted me to do favors like paying a bill but I would smoke up the money. Out of all the substances I have used crack cocaine has been the worse." Byron further explained how he was attracted to women addicted to crack cocaine. They would tempt him to try crack and eventually he gave in to the temptation. Once he tried it the old addictions within him came alive. Byron recalls that while he was in his addiction he lost numerous material things. However, the greatest loss was the love from his family. His focus was clearly on getting the drug by any means necessary. He estimate that within a 3 year period he lost over $100,000 that he earned while hustling on the streets of Philadelphia doing legitimate work. The thing that finally led Byron to his recovery was him catching a moment of sanity while sleeping underground within the subway system. He remembers uttering to some people that he had to get out of the situation that he was in. He entered a drug program and began the long journey to recovery.

He credits his sobriety to actively seeking treatment and believing God to be all-sufficient. He takes one day at a time now and believes that he can fulfill his aspiration by staying clean. He realizes that he can not make up for lost time but what he can do today is be the best person that he can be. Byron is grateful to God and everyone that came into his life helping him to change.

The Love of Her Children was a Catalyst to Recovery

Interview of October 15, 1993

Ann is a 37 year old African American female with seven children and has been free of drugs and alcohol for approximately 6 months. Ann grew up in a single parent home. She lived with her mother, sister and two brothers. She has unpleasant memories of those times being tough because there were times when her family did not have enough to eat. Her brother would steal donuts for them to eat from truck drivers as they made deliveries in the neighborhood.

She talked about her family moving very often leaving her with a feeling of insecurity. She expressed how she at times believed her mother did not love her. Ann felt that her mother cared for her sister more than her. She stated, **"I was always envious of other people and their families."** Ann's family began seeing better times when they were able to move to the southwest section of Philadelphia. Ann reflects on how the better times did not last very long. Her life made an abrupt transformation when she was introduced to drugs at the age of 13. Her peers accepted her and she saw to it that she kept plenty of marijuana in order to maintain her newfound status. It was not too long afterward that she was molested. She then became very promiscuous.

She became pregnant at the age of 15 but was forced to give the child up for adoption. A short time later in her life she was introduced to a substance known as speed which is considered a stimulant. Ann became pregnant for the second time at the age of 18 and moved into her own apartment. A third pregnancy came a short time afterwards. Ann dealt with the struggles of life well. She seemed to possess an inner strength even though she had a weakness for drugs. She and her children's father held jobs, but she still continued to collect welfare and everything seemed to have fallen in place for Ann. What could possibly go wrong? Ann became addicted to crack while her children's father became an alcoholic. In time she began stealing from her job to help feed her habit. She finally returned to her mother's home to live after numerous fights with her children's father. To make matters worse, her sister was also addicted to cocaine.

Ann was gifted with a persuasive gift of conversation and this made it easy for her to obtain the drugs she desired. She was able to get high with city workers who were her senior. Her addiction to crack cocaine was growing rapidly. It was plain to see that Ann's future was on the road to destruction. One of the many occurring tragedies that Ann can recall was the tragedy of her pregnant girlfriend. One day while Ann and her girlfriend were getting high the girlfriend went into labor. Her girlfriend delivered the baby on the couch. Ann and her girlfriend, incredibly, did not seek medical assistance until they were finished smoking their crack cocaine. The baby was born bearing the symptoms of being addicted to crack. As the baby got older it had developed difficulty with normal walking. This was directly attributed to the mother's abuse of cocaine.

Another tragedy that occurred was the time she had a aneurysm in the brain. She recalls vividly receiving her welfare check close to the Easter holiday. She was trying to find the cheapest clothes available so she could have more money to get high. Addicts are extremely ingenious when it comes to budgeting to ensure their severe drug habit will be maintained. She experienced severe headaches while she was smoking crack. The more she smoked the more her head ached. It was as if a series of explosions were going off in her head. In spite of the excruciating pain, the desire to continue to smoke was greater than the concern of pain. Her friends finally placed her on a couch but they continued to get high. No one bothered to seek medical help for her. Smoking crack took precedent over every aspect of her life. Fortunately for Ann, her mother came home and made the phone calls to get her medical help. The hospital discovered that Ann had an aneurysm and they had to operate immediately. The operation was a success but it left Ann with 52 stitches in her head and partially blind. Some people thought this life-threatening event would encourage Ann to turn her life around.

But this event only slowed Ann down. It did not prevent her from getting high. She became angry with her sister and friends because they refused to accept her dependence on drugs. They refused to enable her any longer. However, that did not deter Ann. She was determined to find a way to indulge in her sinister habit. When night arrived, Ann managed to feel her way outside to find her drug dealer who set up shop near her mother's home. She continued to find a way to support her dependency on drugs. She made a miraculous recovery from her operation. The difficulties she was having with her children increased as the vicious cycle of drug addiction continued for Ann. Her living conditions grew worse and she faced the threat of loosing her children to The Department of Human

Services. The fear of loosing her children was the catalyst to begin the journey to recovery. She came into the shelter system to get the help that she badly needed. She relapsed on a few occasions until she finally got things together. Ann began to incorporate the tools and principles she learned into her life.

To help maintain her recovery, Ann attends N.A. (narcotics anonymous) meetings. In addition to N.A. meetings she has sessions with recovery groups and gives talks to people who are serious about living a life of sobriety. Ann, in her conclusion, would like the readers of her story to realize that all the things people think are fun while getting high are no where near the fun you can have living in sobriety. Living a clean life is a celebration within itself. The longer you are clean the longer you will learn to appreciate it. Just take one day at a time.

Intoxicated with Intelligence

Interview of October 17, 1993

Hakim is a 44 year old African American male and at the time of this interview he had been triumphant over his addiction for approximately a year. Hakim was the oldest of 11 children. He remembers experiencing poverty during his childhood. He had to help raise his brothers and sisters which cut his childhood short. It was quite a responsibility of a child of his tender years. Hakim was permanently scarred at the age of 7. He was molested by one of his uncles, but he was reluctant and fearful to reveal this horrible violation of him to anyone.

His mother was a very hard working woman but the City of Philadelphia felt as though she was not doing a good enough job with her children in spite of her efforts. It was not long afterward that Hakim was put in foster care. This breakup of the family prevented Hakim from seeing his brothers and sisters. His mother went to see him while he was in foster care and during one of her visits she noticed that Hakim was smoking cigarettes. His response to his mother when she questioned him as to why he was smoking was, **"I am grown now and I'm on my own."**

Hakim was now moving from foster home to foster home. As a result of these circumstances he was failing in school. The lifestyle that Hakim was now living made it inevitable for him to end up in prison. The drugs, crime and violence that he was involved in spelled greater trouble for Hakim. There were many people who lived similar lifestyles whose fate was equally as unsuccessful as Hakim's, however, he did not learn from their mistakes. Hakim continued to struggle through life and at the age of 17 he left the foster home and ventured out. He was drinking and getting into all sorts of trouble. He had no sense of direction to help guide him in life and predictably, ended up going to prison. Hakim took advantage of the time he spent in prison. He, at last, made a wise decision to go to school. He was finally released after serving a number of years in prison. A short time after his release from prison he found a woman that he settled down with and married. The marriage ended in divorce after 4 years. He resorted to the use of cocaine to compensate for his dismal failure in marriage. His life proceeded on a downhill spiral.

Hakim felt as though he was too smart for anyone to tell him about his misdirected lifestyle. He was too intelligent to stay sober. Many addicts think that they are privy to some special insight that eludes the rest of humanity. To support his habit, he washed cars and became involved in small time hustling. At times he was a lookout person for drug dealers. He makes the point that one of the reasons why it was so hard to fight the war on drugs is the fact that addicts and dealers learn to think like the authorities that are trying to catch them. Hakim eventually became homeless and out of necessity had to live in homeless shelters and subway stations. When times were more severe, he lived in abandoned houses and an occasional doorway. He ate in soup kitchens and wherever he could find a meal. His future seemed doomed to failure.

Hakim describes some of the places where he lived as having 30 entrances and 50 exits. In other words, there were many ways in and many ways out. He use to stay up for days at a time, and as many addicts do he slept only when his body became completely exhausted. He witnessed people being beaten with golf clubs and even shot because of disputes they had with drug dealers. He tells of a man getting shot in the leg while he was still tenaciously holding on to his crack pipe. In another situation, a man in a burning house remained in the conflagration continuing to get high. His fascination for getting high outweighed his desire to preserve his life. The fire fighters had to pull him out of the house. Hakim knew women who abandoned their children while pursuing drugs, it became so commonplace. He also witnessed women performing sex acts on men in order to satisfy their quest for drugs. He explained how an animalistic lifestyle rapidly develops in the life of an addict. It is life with no rules or conventional social standards.

The thing that motivated Hakim to stop using was the realization that he was simply too tired to go on. The people that he knew who had stopped using drugs were an inspiration to him. He really began to seriously deal with himself and re-evaluate his goals in life. He gradually ceased to abuse himself. His therapist commented to him that if someone had abused him the way he abused himself, he would probably contemplate killing such a person.

Today he realizes that the only thing that matters is keeping the Creator first and foremost in his life. He attributes what he has learned through the religion of Al-Islam and the people he met in Narcotics Anonymous as being very helpful to his recovery. He has learned how to trust people again. He is actively involved with groups that are doing positive things to help others suffering from substance abuse. His new philosophy is that one should surround himself with people who have a positive attitude. It took him going through a number of experiences which had a severe impact on his life to realize that: ***Every failure will teach you a lesson that you need to learn if you will keep your eyes as well as your ears open and be willing to be taught. Every adversity can turn out to be a blessing in disguise. Without reverses and temporary defeats you would never know the sort of metal of which you are made of. Finally, he suggests one should take a look at what happens to people who wrongfully use drugs.***

He Would Not Stay Down for The Count

Interview of November 10, 1993

C.B. is a 43-year-old African American male who at the time of this interview had been in rehabilitation for several months. He is a single father of two children. C.B came from a small family, which consisted of his brother and his parents. When he was a juvenile, he was exposed to alcohol and drugs through friends as well as his relatives. He points out how our society is a drug culture and we learn to celebrate everything by drinking. We drink during holidays, when someone is born or when someone dies. He further adds how the human being is a creature of habit. When you do something long enough, it becomes part of you even before you reach the addiction stage. Today, in our society, drugs are very popular and too easily accessible. This fact, according to C.B., helped play a crucial part in his addiction. He experienced more than his share of physical harm at the hands of others as a result of his drug and alcohol environment.

He gives an account of getting into a dispute with a drug dealer and had the temerity to threaten the dealer that he would summon the police. Today C.B. realizes that this could have cost him his life. The drug dealer's associates chased him and beat a change of attitude into him. It was only by the grace of God that he was able to emerge from this situation alive. On another occasion, C.B. got into a confrontation with a male at a party. His opponent, wielding a knife, inflicted severe wounds on him. He seemed to have a progression of misadventures in his life. One of C.B.'s close relatives died drawing him into a prolonged state of depression. His addiction intensified and ultimately he became homeless. This was the juncture in his life where he decided to make some dramatic changes for his benefit. C.B, credits his belief in Al-Islam with helping him greatly in recovering from his addiction. He hit rock bottom numerous times. He learned to get up each time he would fall.

His message is, ***"Look around and see how drug use has destroyed so many lives that had*** *potential before taking such a dangerous path. The nature of alcohol and drugs is failure and destruction. Its nature destroys the human being spiritually, physically and financially. It is the most obvious conclusion. No one has been successful using alcohol or drugs in excess. Every time you wake up you are given another chance. Seek the help from those who can help you. You were not born this way. Keep an open mind. If you fall get up. Pray to the Almighty because your help will ultimately come from God alone."*

Prison- My Road To Recovery

Interview of November 20, 1993

Juan is a 25-year-old Hispanic male who has been drug free for 4 years. He was interviewed while he was serving time in a State Penitentiary. He had a brother and a sister that died at birth. His second sister died as a result of using drugs. He believes what led to his addiction was his desire to be accepted by his peers. His first drug was alcohol and it did not take him long to advance to using heroin. He use to make so much money from drugs that it did not matter to him if he made it to his legal place of employment. Juan expressed to the interviewer how his thoughts became more rational and he began to realize that when doing drugs the initial drug leads to another and another. If it's God will Juan hope to go back with his family.

He reads the Bible now and considers himself a God-fearing man. He can not predict what will happen once he is released from prison but he feels confident that he will not return to his old life of depravity and hopelessness. In conclusion Juan feels that everybody has to learn for himself because people very often do not listen. He gave the analogy of how a mother tells her child not to do a particular thing but the child disobeys. A lot of our people fall into this category, especially the young generation. People sometimes learn from their mistakes. Hopefully the mistakes will not be fatal.

Death of My Beloved

Interview of November 20, 1993

This interview takes place at a State Penitentiary where the next subject, Carlos, was in confinement. He is a 43 year old Hispanic and has been free from illegal substances for approximately 30 months. He states that he was never too close to his family and he does not get along too well with his sister. Even though, his parents were strict, he was the principal member of his family that got into trouble. Carlos believes what led to his addiction to drugs was the type of people he associated with. His first drug was marijuana as is common with many first time offenders. He moved on to other drugs until heroin became his drug of choice. He had a love affair with drugs for 17 years. Drugs were an all-consuming part of his existence. He lost many good jobs and eventually lost his family. One of Carlos' sons also had an addiction despite the fact that he had only one lung due to an illness. Carlos, oblivious to this fact continued to use drugs. Sadly, for his son, death was the only answer to his drug problem. Even, after this tragedy in Carlos life, he continued on his path to destruction. His wife attempted to take his life because of the many problems he was causing her and their family due to unbearable abuse. Carlos began to think about his remaining son and began to realize how he desired to be just like his father. He was in effect his son's role model. It motivated him to reflect on the life he was living. He did not want his son to end up like his brother. This became an encompassing fear. He was setting such a terrible example of how not to live a productive life. He knew that a change had to take place. The death of his son was a major factor, which contributed to his desire for recovery. It was an arduous road.

Today he has the will to do whatever is necessary to teach a better way of life to his son. He hopes that his son understands there are consequences of one's lifestyle. He strongly feels that once his son understands this he will be prepared to live with the choices that he makes in life. Carlos hopes to stay free from drugs once he is release from prison. He is doing his best to live a good life, taking one day at a time. He realizes things will not be easy for him. There are a lot of traps that appear to come into your path once you commit yourself to be drug free. He will continue to strive to please God. He prays that spirit will be his salvation.

Eyewitness to Death- One Antidote for Addiction

Interview of November 20, 1993

Bill is a 44 year old Caucasian male and at the time of this interview he had been sober for 8 years. Bill was confined to a State Penitentiary during the time this interview took place. He was the third child in a family of six. His grandparents raised him since he was one week old. He was born a blue baby and was very sickly. (A blue baby is a baby that is born suffering with a heart defect.) He was 3½ years of age before he met his immediate family for the first time. His father was an officer in the

U.S. Navy and some of the family traveled with him. He did drugs for the first time in 1966. The drugs were marijuana and LSD. He was a talented guitarist in a band from the time he was in high school until he joined the army in 1968. The culture he identified himself with experimented with drugs continually. In the year 1969 he graduated to using a large amount of heroin and cocaine. He was involved with a motorcycle club that accepted the illegal use as a staple in their diet. He can recall seeing people fall over and die from using narcotics as a common occurrence. He lost the desire to use drugs after seeing so many people die. This was a gradual process.

Today he finds drug use to be offensive and does not desire to be remotely a part of the drug scene. His experiences have taught him a great lesson in drug addiction. He was explicit that it was only by God's grace he survived. The good values that his grandparents taught him he hope to apply to his life when he is released from incarceration. He increasingly draws upon what they taught him as a child nowadays. He is making good use of his time in constructive ways and hopefully he will prevent repeating the mistakes he made in the past.

How Paula defeated the Burn-Out of Life

Interview of June 9, 1994

Paula is a single 28 year old African American female. She was drug free for approximately six months when she gave this interview. Paula relates that both of her parents were alcoholics and the environment she grew up in was surrounded with alcoholics. She vividly remembers her mother putting beer in her baby bottle while she was only 3 years of age. She continued to drink as she got older. Paula's mother had many boyfriends. She was raped by one of them when she was very young. Her mother told her boyfriend to leave the house after Paula revealed this horrendous act to her. However, the man was allowed to return after only two weeks. This caused Paula to have a great deal of hatred towards her mother. Paula carried these feelings with her until she became much older and began therapy. Years later she began using cocaine and it was not long before she became heavily addicted. She describes the high as the feeling one gets when you feel you are problem free. In reality the problems appear to have disappeared, but after the high wears off the problems are looking you square in the face.

She would always try to suppress her true feelings by using drugs. Paula stated she had been on the receiving end of many violent assaults because of her custom of trying to swindle someone with the purpose to feed her habit. As a dealer, sometimes she would substitute baking soda and soap in the place of drugs in order to finalize a drug deal. She did not care what happened to others because she had only her selfish interest at heart. If her boyfriend had cocaine, she would steal it from him when he went to the bathroom or had fallen asleep. She would not worry about the consequences of her actions. The only priority in Paula's life was getting high!

On many occasions, her boyfriend would beat her mercilessly for stealing his supply of drugs, but that did not deter her. She seemed to be equally addicted to the challenge of stealing. Her appetite was never satisfied. She remembers one of her friends being beaten with a baseball bat for stealing drugs that belonged to his associates. It was a blessing that she survived. She can recall how she would look on the floor for the crumbs of cocaine, which in reality were not there. Paula clearly recollects what finally persuaded her to choose an alternative lifestyle. On one occasion while using drugs, she felt burnt out, unable to talk, move or catch her breath. She had never experience this level of fear before. This was the crucial turning point in her life. She was about to lose her children when a blessing from God made it possible for her to get the assistance she so urgently needed if not deserved. She understood drastic changes had to take place in her life in order to save her children. She now attends Narcotic

Anonymous meetings and has a sponsor. She also has learned she must not allow anything to interfere with her recovery. In conclusion, her message for the reader is, ***"You do not have to use anymore. Get in touch with people who have found a positive way to live. Be open-minded to helpful suggestions, make meetings everyday, pray and believe that there is a power greater than yourself. This greater power will help you get through any trying moment so you will not have to rely on drugs."*** Paula feels that if she was to start using again she would die. This mind-set helps her to stay focused on what she must do for herself and her children.

Without Hope, There are No Choices

Interview of June 20, 1994

Pam is a 35-year African American female who has celebrated sobriety for 17 months. She came from what may be considered a middle class family. Her mother was a nurse and her father a postal worker. Her father died during the early part of 1994. Pam speaks of taking her first drink while she was at a summer camp in New York. She tells a story of a young counselor who gave her and several other children some alcohol to drink. Pam explained that at the age of 14 there were an abundance of pills for various problems in the

55

home. She was introduced to marijuana and other drugs while she was attending school in a suburban community. Her biggest enticement at the time was marijuana, which she used up to age 19. She became bored using marijuana and wanted to try something more exciting. That something more exciting turned out to be cocaine and methamphetamines. Pam had her first child at the age of 23. She was introduced to cocaine by a new acquaintance. Because of Pam's dependence on cocaine, she lost her job and in time she lost her home. Pam lost what little dignity she had left when she as a last resort turned to prostitution to support her habit. Pam mother took her daughter away from her while she was living this unstable lifestyle. She continued using drugs even though tragedies were occurring in her life.

She was addicted to that awesome high that many addicts strive for and inevitably became a slave to. Pam compares being on drugs to someone sinking into a dark pit while trying desperately to swim free. It is cold and lonely. If you don't tread the water, you will drown.

Pam experienced many scary moments while she was in her addiction. One of the things she can recall was holding a stillborn baby in her arms while she was using cocaine. On one occasion, she remembers being gagged and raped by her assailants. She also tells of her leg being broken by an aggressor. She contracted venereal diseases on several occasions. There were instances in which she had guns drawn on her as a result of her own aggressive behavior towards others. Violence and aggression are common- place in the drug world. Pam pointed out that no matter how many drugs you take you feel as though you need more. Your world becomes a bottomless pit. The feeling of being high for her was a sensation greater than sex. Pam went on to say that most addicts are very loquacious and have a great deal of charisma when it comes to their conversation. They can be quite persuasive in their world of deception.

The events that took place in Pam's life played a major role in encouraging her decision to discontinue using drugs. She knew she had to surrender herself to God, nothing else worked for her. This was her only hope. Pam had finally reached the point in her life where she did not want to use any form of narcotics.

Pam puts it this way, *"I pray a lot and Jesus gets me through the moment. I cried out for Jesus to help me and he does. I'm clean today. My children are clean and cared for and I'm back to work. I have dreams I know I can reach. Not only have I saved my life but I have saved my soul."* In conclusion, Pam's message to those who are using drugs or who may be thinking about using is, *"Don't do it but expose it. Drop to your knees and give God a chance. Education is a real big key and you can do anything that you really want to do. There is life after death. Get it together. In the blink of an eye we will be gone. It's that quick."*

The Ultimate Defeat

Interview of June 26, 1994

Martisha is a 40 year old single African American female. At the time of this interview she had successfully completed 25 months in recovery. She grew up in a good, stable family. Her parents set a good example for her and other family members. Martisha along with her six siblings became addicted to drugs at a very young age. She later became involved with a man who was very violent. He was especially violent when they got high together. On one occasion, she thought she would have to jump out of a window to get away from him, during one violent episode. It was a blessing from God that he stopped his assault on her. Due to his deranged frame of mind, there was no way of knowing what he would have done. She had to be admitted to the hospital for the injuries she sustained. She was able to stay strong long enough to stop getting high. This only lasted for 60 days and she then returned to her dangerous way of life. Her boyfriend picked up where he left off. This time he bludgeoned her with a lead pipe while they were getting high.

Martisha continued to stay with her boyfriend irrespective of the danger it posed for herself. The turning point in her life came when she began experiencing the loss of many things close to her. The lost of her home and her children caused her to feel defeated. It was at that moment she decided to try Church. She prayed to God to give her the strength to be freed from the enslavement of drugs. Her life then became filled with positive things. She became serious about life and now has people in her life that give her strong support. One of her strongest supporters was her father. Although he passed away, she did not allow this to discourage her from making progress in life. She keeps her father's memory alive and that helps her to endure. She has a new man in her life that cares for her and her family. She was blessed with a new home. She now detaches herself from people she in the past got high with and stays around positive thinking people.

Her message for the reader is simply this: *Do not use drugs because it could create a traumatic change in your life. Ask for help and tell someone today that you want to live. Don't pick up the drug or drink because one often leads to the next. Pray and be sincere. Stay away from people who don't want what you want in life.*

The Power of the Congregation

Interview of August 26, 1994

Samantha is a 37-year-old African American female that has been living a life free of the influence of drugs for 16 months. She spent a lot of time with relatives who were a poor influence on her impressionable young life. Their pastime was spent in the alcohol and drug scene. Her parents were separated when she was just a tot. They had joint custody of her. She spent equal time with her parents. Her father had a drinking problem; therefore, she had ample opportunity to sample his alcohol when he was not at home. She was approximately 17 years of age when she began to drink frequently. She advanced to marijuana as time moved on. She says one of the greatest tragedies in her life was when some men raped her. This resulted in her being hospitalized. This ordeal drew her into a deep state of depression. The men were arrested for the assault. She had to face the very same men that raped her while she was going back and forth to court. This was an extremely trying ordeal for her. She eventually had antidepressant medication prescribed for her. It was not long afterward that she met a new acquaintance who introduced her to cocaine. In the beginning, Samantha snorted cocaine but later resorted to smoking it. She has a vivid recollection of seeing a man overdosing from the use of heroin. Some of the people that were on the scene at the time removed the needle from the man's arm and dragged him outside of the *"shooting gallery"* where the man eventually died shortly thereafter.

Samantha tells the story of seeing a girl attacked by a man with a baseball bat while the girl was in her addiction. It escapes her memory what prompted the attack. On one occasion she took so many drugs that it caused her to become so delusional that she had to be treated with medication to bring her back to normal. She often blacked out on the streets because of her drug use. She believes it was only by the grace of God that she was able to survive the many ordeals that she subjected herself to. Her mother was very supportive of her. On numerous occasions she cared for her children while she was living an irresponsible life. She would leave her children with her for weeks at a time while she was battling her drug problem. Samantha spoke of an incident where a man was violently attacked while in a drug house. The man later died from head injuries that he sustained from this senseless, vicious assault. She witnessed and was a participant of more acts of violence than a combat infantryman. At least the infantryman has a cause.

Samantha was very scared but not scared enough to stop using drugs. It was during this period that she received a nice sum of money from her income tax return. She was living extravagantly for a while. She continued smoking cocaine and became very paranoid.

She was so paranoid she actually thought she was dying. She was taken to the hospital and miraculously they were able to bring her back to normal. She was at a stage in her life where she did not believe she could ever stop using drugs. Samantha, despite her lifestyle with drugs, remained connected with the Church that she joined earlier in her life. Her Church continued throughout the years to be supportive of her in her misguided journey. The Pastor made it clear that the Church would be there for her no matter what the circumstances were. He would often send for her to come to Church and was persistent with his effort. On one occasion, he sent for her and told the members of the Church not to leave until Samantha came with them. The wall of fear, hatred and resentment made it difficult for her to surrender, because she was having a hard time dealing with the tragedy of being raped. It was a blessing from God that Samantha had the kind of supportive members of her Church and the hospital workers that helped her. Samantha has never forgotten the support that she was blessed to receive. She made a decision to go into the shelter system until she could bring some semblance of order to her life. She somehow succeeded to obtain her very own place. This was a major accomplishment for her. She now occasionally goes to Narcotics Anonymous meetings and remains very close to her Church. The Church became the foundation for her strength to succeed. The people she associate with today do not use drugs and are good company. Her faith in God is strong and she keeps God first and foremost in her life today. Her message is: ***There is no such thing that you can not stop using drugs. You can not stop using for your mother or your children. You have to do it for yourself. You may make a mistake but you have to realize everybody is not successful on their first try. To the people who are thinking about using, just be conscious of the people that you hang around. Be mindful of what you do. You don't have to be in with the crowd to survive.***

An Inner Voice- the Road to Recovery

Interview of June 6, 1995

Jewel is a 36 year old African American female with two young adult children. She had been in recovery for seven years when she was interviewed. Jewel came from a family of eight brothers and sisters. They were separated from their mother at a very early age because her mother had a serious drinking problem. They subsequently were placed in different foster homes. Thereafter, for years they had very little contact. She never really knew her father, therefore, had no significant male role model in her life. Jewel had a difficult time making the adjustment to her changed environment. She returned home to her mother at the age of 11 but still she could not adjust to her mother's lifestyle. This predicament made it necessary for her to become street smart and rather clever. This did not prevent her from becoming twice pregnant. Although she was a single parent with two children, she made an attempt to complete her education while working full time.

Jewel recounted coming up as a black woman she attempted to do a lot of positive things. She was the unwitting victim of much abuse. She got into a relationship with a young man she met. Although the relationship was tumultuous and abusive, some good, ironically, came out of it. He helped to find her way out of the projects. This, at first, appeared to be a step in the right direction, but as time went on this situation turned her dream into a hellish nightmare. Jewel finally made a decision to get out of this situation before things became too critical. She moved into the home of a sister whom she was very close to. On one unforgettable evening, her beloved sister was discovered dead on the sofa in her home. This was very devastating to Jewel because of the closeness that she shared with her sister. She began to associate with people who were doing drugs and it was not long before drugs became an integral part of her life. She, at first, began snorting cocaine and later progressed to smoking crack cocaine. She was now addicted to crack and found herself doing things that she never dreamed she would have done to support her addiction. She describes being on drugs as one being a slave to a mental and physical death, a living hell. You become a prisoner of your warped mind and tormented body. Crack had Jewel captured and her life was under total siege. She felt trapped with no sense of rescue. There appeared to be no way out. She thought she would be an addict until the day she died. That in itself was a fate worse than death.

Jewel was forever angry while she was using drugs. She had blamed everything on God because of her weakness. She was not ready to accept responsibility for her actions. One evening she met a man while she was wandering the streets. She made a proposition to him in order to get some money to support her habit. They went to an abandoned area in the neighborhood where she began unbuttoning her shorts. The man assaulted her repeatedly. He, to her dismay, did not desire her sexual favors. He seemed more interested in inflicting pain on Jewel. She later understood this was obviously about his control over her. The man knocked out one of her teeth and bruised her body very badly. She envisioned death approaching her. Today she realizes it was only by the grace of God that she was able to survive this horror. One would think that the first stop for Jewel would have been the police, but Jewel's quest for the crack was more urgent. She ended up in a crack house. The people that saw her after this ordeal thought for certain that she had been raped. The story she revealed to them was unimaginable. It was not too long after this incident that she ended up going to a shelter in Philadelphia for adults and children. While she was in the shelter someone gave her twenty dollars to make a purchase at a local store. Jewel never made it to the store. She encountered an old friend and they were off on an adventure to buy drugs. Jewel had stayed away for so long that the Department of Human Services was called to take custody of her children. She was fortunate that her children were able to get in touch with one of her brothers. He provided temporary care for them. She recalls that she had come to a point in her life where she was not at all pleased with herself as a mother. She saw herself as a complete failure. She was very angry and unhappy with herself. Her heart became heavy. She finally came to the place in her life whereby she had grown weary of being the

76

person she had become. She mulled over in her mind the possibility of committing suicide. It was at this moment she heard a clear voice that said, *"You have tried everything else why not try God."*

Jewel understood the reality of what she had heard and began to make positive changes in her wretched life. To maintain her sobriety Jewel chose not to be around people who were drug users. She presently attends meetings and only associates with people who have a similar philosophy for life. Her reasoning is simplistic. She states that if she does not pick up the drug she can not get high. Jewel's message for anyone using drugs is simply this: *Give yourself a break and get help. Surrender to your higher power. Don't wait until it is too*

late. If the drugs don't get you, aids will. Life is beautiful!

She Knew She Was Destined to Perish without a Lifestyle Change

Interview of July 1, 1995

Susan is a single parent with two children. During this interview, Susan, a 37-year-old Caucasian female had been triumphant in her recovery for 7 years. She was raised in a small town in the state of Ohio. She felt that she never really fitted in with her peers and found herself to be unhappy. She took her first drink at the age of 14. She believes what lead her to drink was her desire to be accepted by her peers, as do many youths. She became introduced to heroin by the time she was 15 and became an intravenous drug user. Susan quit school while she was in the 10th grade and at the age of seventeen she left home. She somehow thought her drug use was glamorous. She thought, in her words, **"it was loads of fun."** Drug use was a way of life for her. She lived to use and used to live. She describes herself as being the walking dead while she was in her addiction. She remembers one of the biggest tragedies happening to her in her addiction was when her husband died from a drug overdose. She later found out that she was HIV positive. Susan then had reached a point in her life that she could no longer tolerate the way she was living. It was only a matter of time before some type of change had to take place before she would end her life.

She had reached a point in her life where she was compelled to do something about her drug use. She admitted herself into a rehabilitation center and has been making steady progress since that time. Susan is very active in the 12 Step program of Narcotics Anonymous. She makes it a habit to faithfully attend the meetings. She knew it was imperative to disassociate herself from people who are not serious about living a drug free life. Her message for anyone who is thinking about using drugs is: **Say *no and don't get started. Pray for people who are already on drugs. Encourage them to seek a better way of life. They have a choice. There was a time I did not believe in God, but today God is very much a part of my life.***

Tariq Adib Shabazz

Conclusion

Drug addiction continues to present itself as a major problem in our society. It continues to destroy untold members of our society. Some of the best minds available to us today can only come up with theories and conjectures when it comes to practical solutions to this crisis. It is amazing how many people miraculously recover from drug and alcohol addiction when it appeared that their lives were headed for total destruction. On the other hand, we find the people who lives appeared to be promising come to an end as a result of falling victim to the drug plague. Many people have reached conclusions on how to solve the drug problem. Some have joined 12 step programs. Others have joined Churches, Mosques and other religious establishments. Why one method works for some and not for others is a question that still has many puzzled. Why some people will go through the most bizarre extremes to satisfy their craving for drugs and alcohol remains a mystery. Perhaps it's the lure of the forbidden fruit.

I am of the opinion that it will take a combination of all the successful methods to help with this drug crisis along with a sincere commitment to the Creator. We could spend countless hours debating which method is better to deal with the drug crisis or which opinion should be accepted. Ideally, we would like things to be a certain way, but realistically we have to accept the fact that things are not the way we would like them to be. Rhetoric will not solve the problems. Prayers without work are not realistic. With the help of the Creator and the serious minded, committed individuals working together to solve this crisis perhaps we will make progress in dealing with this devastating plague. Finally, I will close in the words of a wise philosopher who stated, ***"We grow because we struggle. We learn and we overcome."***